PLAYS FOR PERFORMANCE

*A series designed for
contemporary production and study
Edited by
Nicholas Rudall and Bernard Sahlins*

EURIPIDES

The Trojan Women

In a New Translation by
Nicholas Rudall

Ivan R. Dee
CHICAGO

Library of Congress Cataloging-in-Publication Data:
Euripides.
    [Trojan women.   English]
    The Trojan women / Euripides ; in a new translation by Nicholas Rudall.
       p.   cm. — (Plays for performance)
    ISBN 1-56663-223-4 (acid-free paper). —
ISBN 1-56663-224-2 (pbk. : acid-free paper)
      1. Hecuba (Legendary character)—Drama. 2. Queens—Troy (Extinct city)—Drama. 3. Trojan War—Drama.
I. Rudall, Nicholas. II. Title. III. Series.
PA3975.T8R83   1999
882'.01—dc21   99-21034

INTRODUCTION
by Nicholas Rudall

The Trojan Women was performed in 415 B.C. at ~~fertility, madness, wine~~ Athens, in the theatre of Dionysus, before an audience of citizens who were in the midst of a devastating war. The plays of the Athenian dramatists were performed only once. This simple fact gave the plays a distinct political significance. Not only were they performed before the citizen body as a whole in a single event, but there was also an accepted sense that the playwrights of Athens were the city-state's principal conscience. Athens was a *polis*, and the plays were truly *political.*

One year before the performance of *The Trojan Women*, Athens had invaded the island of Melos, which was Greek but determinedly neutral in the war between Athens and Sparta, the Peloponnesian War. Athenian forces captured the island, put its men to death, and enslaved its women and children. This barbaric act provoked the people of Athens. Thucydides, for example, included in his history a debate on the moral dilemma raised by the invasion. It is clear that Euripides' *Trojan Women* enters into this debate, but it is much more an elemental condemnation of war than a tactical or philosophical argument. We are thrust into the presence of the pain of innocent victims of war. What makes Euripides' case so compelling is that the women whom we meet are Trojans: they are the "barbarians." The oppressors are Greeks: they are

3

the "civilized." In a very real sense, Euripides forces his audience to see its own heroes—the victors of Troy and the great figures of the Iliad, Agamemnon, Odysseus, and Menelaus—as cowards who kill and enslave helpless women and children.

The play is virtually without action. The women of Troy are paraded before us in all their grief and humiliation. Hecuba rises from the ground and sings a dirge on the fall of Troy and the death of her husband. Her daughter, Cassandra, maddened by sorrow and by her rape at the hands of Agamemnon, dances onto the stage in a frenzy. Suddenly her prophetic gifts chillingly tell of her own and other deaths. Andromache enters with her infant son, Astyanax, who is torn from her arms to be thrown to his death from the city walls. Then there is a strange and almost comic trial of Helen, conducted by Hecuba in the presence of Menelaus. The scene purports to condemn Helen for her infidelity and her instigation of the war. But the Greek audience must have been aware of the irony, for they knew that Helen and Menelaus would go home and live happily ever after. As husband and wife leave, the women of Troy are left to mourn the deaths of their husbands and sons, to contemplate their own impending slavery, and to watch their city burn.

Much of the original play was intended to be sung. Within the conventions of Greek drama, singing or chanting intensified the emotional impact. Spoken dialogue was reserved for intellectual argument and exposition. The Trojan Women contains proportionally more singing than any other Greek tragedy. This is not to suggest that a modern production should copy ancient conventions, but for reference, within the text I have marked those places where the singing occurred. As always in this

4

Plays for Performance series, this translation was composed with performance in mind. Individual characters have specific speech patterns. For example, Talthybius, the Greek messenger, is a common man with predominantly simple and direct diction; Hecuba is dignified and lyrical; Cassandra is alternately lucid and obscure; Menelaus is a not very intelligent military man. The chorus of captive Trojan women has a deeply melodic tone. Their poetry is at once beautiful and harsh. The words I have given the characters are meant to be spoken by contemporary actors, and I have tried to make these words as clear and concise as possible. And I have attempted to translate what was, of course, contemporary Greek for its ancient audience into contemporary English for a modern audience.

The first production of this translation was performed at the Shakespeare Theatre in Washington, D.C. JoAnne Akalaitis, the play's director, chose to set the play in a water-stained, crumbling concrete holding cell. The Trojan women had their heads shaved; the Greek soldiers wore modern police uniforms and helmets which hid their faces and rendered them frightening and anonymous. By a coincidence of history, the first performance took place when images of the victims of Kosovo were entering the American conscience. The timelessness of this great tragedy was palpable.

5

CHARACTERS

POSEIDON, God of the Sea, brother of Zeus
ATHENA, patron goddess of Athens, daughter of Zeus
HECUBA, wife of Priam, king of Troy, and mother of
  Hector, Cassandra, and Polyxena
TALTHYBIUS, a Greek herald
CASSANDRA, daughter of Priam and Hecuba
ANDROMACHE, wife of Hector
MENELAUS, king of Sparta, husband of Helen
HELEN, wife of Menelaus, daughter of Zeus
CHORUS of Trojan women

The Trojan Women

angry

POSEIDON: I am Poseidon, God of the Sea, Shaker of
the Earth.
I have come from the depths where the Nereids
dance their grace
In the eddies of the Aegean sea. I love this city of
Troy.
Apollo and I ringed it with high walls of stone,
and I have kept it nestled in my heart's core.
But now smoke rises slow from its ruins, burned
and flattened by the army of the Greeks.
They built a wooden horse within whose womb
they hid an army,
Sent it within my loved walls—an artifact of
death.
Epeus did this. Athena devised the plan. It will
live in history.
Now the sacred places of the gods are silent, the
temple walls weep blood,
And at the altar where he worshiped and prayed
for deliverance, King Priam lies dead.
The Greeks have robbed the city of its wealth, are
loading gold into their ships,
And now they wait, wait only for a favoring
breeze to send them home.
After ten long years they will laugh again in the
arms of their wives, their children.

I will leave my city, my Troy.
I am defeated. Hera, lover of Greeks, Athena,
hater of Trojans,
Have driven me from the altars where I was worshiped.

11

The devastation of my city has left the temples empty, and all respect has died.

The river banks of Scamander echo with the deafening screams of the young women of Troy.

They are assigned to their new masters by a throw of dice.

Arcadia takes some. Thessaly takes some. Athens takes some.

But here in these tents the most desirable prizes wait for their Greek masters:

Helen, a slave now as is right, waits.

Hecuba, that queen of grief, waits.

She lies before the gates of Troy and weeps.

She does not know that her daughter Polyxena is most foully dead

And lies beside Achilles' tomb. Her husband Priam is dead, all her children too.

All but Cassandra. Apollo made her mad but preserved her virginity.

Now against all human feelings and laws divine she has been raped.

King Agamemnon took her by force.

So I leave. Farewell my once so glorious Troy. Farewell you walls of polished stone.

If Athena, daughter of Zeus, had not chosen your destruction, you would be standing still.

(enter Athena)

ATHENA: Poseidon, you are my father's brother, a powerful and respected god.

May I put an end to our quarrel and speak to you?

POSEIDON: Queen Athena, you may. You are my family, and the ties of blood are strong.

ATHENA: I thank you for your kindness. I have a plan
that you and I should talk about.

POSEIDON: Some instructions from Olympus, perhaps? From Zeus or from some other god?

ATHENA: No. This is about Troy. I have come to seek
your help for this land where we now stand.

POSEIDON: Have you laid aside your former hatred?
Perhaps you feel some compassion for this city,
now that it is burnt to ashes?

ATHENA: Let me repeat: I seek your help. Will you
help me fulfill my plans?

POSEIDON: I will. But tell me whom you wish to
help—Greeks or Trojans?

ATHENA: The Trojans I once hated. Now I wish them *disregard consequence*
joy.
But for the Greeks, I want their journey home to
be one of suffering. *change of mood*

POSEIDON: You shift from mood to mood. Why?
Your love and your hate, no matter the object,
both go too far.

ATHENA: Have you not heard of the outrage done to
me and my holy temples?

POSEIDON: I have. Ajax dragged Cassandra from your
altar by force.

ATHENA: Yes. And the Greeks did nothing, said nothing.

POSEIDON: But it was with *your* help and strength that
they sacked Troy.

ATHENA: *That* is why I want to join with you to do
them harm.

POSEIDON: My power is yours to command. What is your plan?

ATHENA: I will fill their journey home with pain.

POSEIDON: When they are still on land or when they are at sea?

ATHENA: Whenever they set sail for home, Zeus will send torrents of rain and hail,
Hurricanes that will turn the heavens black.
He says he will give me the fire of his thunderbolts to strike their ships and set them all ablaze.
You must do your part.
Make the Aegean Sea roar with monstrous waves that crash and churn the deep.
Fill the sheltering bays of Euboea with the bodies of the drowned.
The Greeks must learn to live in awe of my shrines and to respect every other god.

POSEIDON: It shall be done. You need speak no more. I shall stir the depths of the Aegean Sea.
The shores of Mykonos, the rocky bays of Delos, Scyros, and Lemnos, the reefs of Caphareion
Will be glutted with the corpses of drowned men.
But go to Olympus, take your father's thunderbolts in your hands.
Wait for the moment when they launch their ships.

(exit Athena)

POSEIDON: The man who sacks cities and desecrates temples and the holy tombs of the dead is mad. His own doom is merely . . . waiting.

100   *(exit Poseidon)*

14

(Hecuba begins to rise from the ground. [This dirge was sung.])

HECUBA: Up, sad heart! Raise your head from the
     ground.
Lift your face to the sun.
Troy is no more, the kings of Troy are no more.
Fortunes are ever-changing. Be brave!
Drift with the current, drift with the winds of
     Fate.
Do not steer your ship of life headlong into the
     waves
Which drown the heart.
I weep, I weep. What else can I do?
My country is lost, my children, my husband are
     lost.
The billowing glory of my ancestors is torn to
     shreds
And has come to nothing.
What should I say, what leave unspoken?
This hard ground is my bed.
My limbs lie heavy on the pitiless earth.
My head, my temples, my sides throb in pain.
I long to stretch my spine
And sway from side to side
To the rhythm of my endless tears.
For grief is the music of the wretched of the
     earth:
We chant the sad dirges of our doom.

From Greece across the deep, dark sea
The ships sailed safe to Troy.
Beating their oars to the hateful blare of trum-
     pets
And the soft whistling of flutes.
Here in our waters they dropped anchor.

They came for Helen, loathsome wife of
    Menelaus,
Who brought shame upon her brothers,
Shame upon her city,
And death to Priam, my husband,
Father of fifty sons.

She brought the disaster of doom to me,
    Hecuba.

Out there is Agamemnon's tent.
I sit and wait to be taken as a slave
From my home.
I am old.
My head is naked in its grief.

Oh women of Troy!
Widows of the valiant dead,
Sad maidens, unhappy wives!
Troy smolders in ruins.
Let us weep for Troy.
I am like some mother bird
That protects her young.

I shall begin the dirge.

How different from the times
I once sang to the gods
As I leaned upon King Priam's staff
And beat my foot to the rhythm
Of the Trojan pipe.

(enter Chorus A) [The Chorus can be divided into
two parts: Chorus A and B, perhaps young and
old. I have made some suggestions of possible assignments. The chorus also sang or chanted this
interchange with Hecuba.]

CHORUS LEADER A: Hecuba! Why these cries? These
    screams of pain?
  What news has come? Your lamentations echoed
    along the palace walls.
  Terror seizes the heart of every Trojan woman,
    slaves now in their grief.

HECUBA: My child, even now the Greek ships are . . .

CHORUS WOMAN A1: Are the rowers at their oars?

CHORUS WOMAN A2: What does this mean?

CHORUS WOMAN A3: The time has come! Will they
    take me from my home?

HECUBA: I do not know, but I feel the end is near.

LEADER A: Women of Troy! Cassandra! Come to us,
    come hear your doom!
  The Greeks are setting sail!

HECUBA: Oh do not call upon Cassandra. She is
    mad.
  Do not expose her to the mockery of Greeks.
  Oh grief upon grief! Oh Troy, sad Troy, you are
    nothing now!
  Oh sad children of this land, living and dead. You
    are nothing now.

(Chorus B enters)

CHORUS LEADER B: Alas . . . I tremble, my Queen!
  I have come from Agamemnon's tent to hear
    your words.
  Have the Greeks made their decision?
  Will they kill me now or are the sailors on deck
    ready to depart?

HECUBA: My child, steel your heart for pain.

CHORUS WOMAN B1: I have come in terror. Has a herald already come from the Greeks?

CHORUS WOMAN B2: To whom will I be given as a slave?

HECUBA: They are casting lots. Soon you will know.

CHORUS WOMAN B3: Ahhh . . . will it be a man from Argos, or from Phthia, or the Islands?
Who will take me from my home? I weep.

HECUBA: Who will make me his slave? I am old, weak, the mere shadow of a corpse.
Where will I go? I, who once was Queen of Troy,
Will keep watch at someone's gate or be a nurse to children.

[The following lines of both Chorus A and B, who now are joined together, can be individually assigned.]

CHORUS: —Alas, your tears burn deep. I pity you!
—No more will I sit before the loom, here in my beloved home.
—For the last time I look upon the bodies of my children.
—For the last time . . .
—But my sorrows will multiply, forced to lie at night in the bed of a Greek.
—I curse that night and the God that made it so!
—I shall be a bearer of water from the sacred spring of Pirene, slave that I am.
—I pray that I be sent to the land of Theseus, holy Athens.
—Never, never to Argos, hateful home of Helen.
Let me not be a slave to Menelaus,
The sacker of Troy!

18

—Beneath Olympus is a land rich in grain and
  fruit,
Nurtured to beauty by sweet waters. There let me
  live if Athens,
Holy land of Theseus, is denied to me!
—Sicily! Mother of mountains, land of Etna and
  Hephaestos!
I know its fame, have heard of its courage!
—Cross the Ionian Sea, and there is the land
  washed by the sacred waters of Crathis,
Waters that turn the hair to gold, a land rich in
  heroes!   200

CHORUS LEADER: Look! Here is the herald from the
  Greek army!
In haste he brings his store of proclamations.
  What will he tell us? What will his orders be?
For now we are mere slaves to Greek masters.

(enter Talthybius)

TALTHYBIUS: Hecuba! I am Talthybius.
As you know, I made many journeys to Troy as
  messenger of our army.
I have known you a long time. I have the latest
  proclamations.

(Talthybius speaks, but Hecuba sings all her replies)

HECUBA: Ah, women of Troy! This is what we have all
  feared.

TALTHYBIUS: The assignments have been made—if
  that was what you feared.

HECUBA: Ah, where are we to go? Thessaly? Phthia?
  Thebes?

TALTHYBIUS: Each soldier selected his prize individually. You will belong to separate masters.

HECUBA: Who got whom? Can any woman here consider herself lucky?

TALTHYBIUS: I can answer you. But you must ask your questions one at a time.

HECUBA: Then tell me, who got my poor daughter, Cassandra?

TALTHYBIUS: King Agamemnon took her for himself.

HECUBA: To be a slave to his Spartan wife? Alas, alas!

TALTHYBIUS: No, she is to be his mistress and share his midnight bed.

HECUBA: His mistress? She is Apollo's virgin . . . the golden god made her inviolate forever!

TALTHYBIUS: Agamemnon desires her, longs to share her frenzy.

HECUBA: Oh my daughter!
Throw away the holy branches, the protective wreaths that make you safe!

TALTHYBIUS: Why? He is a great king. There will be glory for her in his love.

HECUBA: And my other daughter? The one you took from me?

TALTHYBIUS: Polyxena? That's who you mean?

HECUBA: Yes. To whom was she given?

TALTHYBIUS: She will serve at Achilles' tomb.

HECUBA: Ahh . . . I am the mother of a dead man's slave! My friend, what Greek custom is this?

TALTHYBIUS: May the gods bless your child. She is at peace.

HECUBA: What are you saying? Tell me, is she still alive?

TALTHYBIUS: She is in the hands of Fate. Her troubles are over.

HECUBA: And what of Andromache, brave-hearted Hector's wife? Tell me of her.

TALTHYBIUS: Achilles' son took her—a special prize.

HECUBA: Whose slave am I to be? I, who need a stick to support this ancient body?

TALTHYBIUS: Odysseus, King of Ithaca, took you for his slave.

HECUBA: Ahhh . . . beat your grieving head upon the ground. Tear your cheeks with your nails.
Ahhh . . . I am to be slave to a treacherous, loathsome man who knows no sense of justice,
Who fears no laws of man.
His double-tongue knows only how to lie and shift from this to that,
From that to this. He turns friendship into hatred. Oh weep for me, you Trojan women!
I go to my doom. My fate is the cruelest of all. I am lost forever.

CHORUS: My Queen, you know your fate. But what of me?
What man of Argos or of Thessaly will be my master?

TALTHYBIUS: Bring Cassandra here to me at once!
I will hand her over to Agamemnon and then come back for the rest of the . . . assignments.
What are those flames over there? What are the women doing . . . setting fire to the tents?

21

Are they burning themselves to death because
  they are being shipped to Greece?
The love of freedom lies deep in the heart. They
  will not easily submit to their fate.
Open up! Death may be what they wish, but that
  would not sit well with the Greek army.
Open up! I will not take the blame for this.

HECUBA: There is no fire. It is my daughter, Cassandra.
In her madness she comes rushing here.

*(Enter Cassandra, carrying a torch. She believes she is
about to be married in Apollo's Temple.)* [This first
section was also sung.]

CASSANDRA: Raise the torch on high, bring it to me!
  Ahhh . . . I worship you, my God!
I flood this temple with light. . . . Oh look, look! Oh
  Hymen, God of Marriage,
Blessed is the bridegroom. Blessed am I, bride of a
  royal bed.
I will be married in Argos, Oh Hymen, God of Mar-
  riage!
My mother, I know you weep in lamentations deep
  for my father lost and my fatherland lost.
I myself will carry this torch at my wedding . . . carry
  it into the light of the sun.
Hymen, I will make it blaze for you and for you,
  Hecate,
As is the custom at a virgin's wedding.
Now raise your foot! Lead the dance of joy! Evoi!
  Evoi! Sing out!
I feel now as I did in my father's time, in days of
  pure happiness.
The dance is holy. Apollo, lead the dance! Here in
  your temple, amongst the laurel trees,

I am your priestess. Oh Hymen, God of Marriage!
Dance, mother!
Laugh to the skies! Dance with me, step by step,
now here, now there.
Oh dance your love for me! Greet the bride,
mother, cry aloud!
Let there be songs and cries of joy. Come, you Tro-
jan maids, in your loveliest robes.
Sing at my wedding, sing to the husband that fate
brings to my bed.

CHORUS: My Queen, take her in your arms.
Stop her madness or she will dance into the cruel
arms of the Greeks.

[From here until the next Choral Ode, everyone
speaks. There is no singing.]

HECUBA: Oh God of Fire! Yes, you light the torches
of mortal weddings, but it was cruel to set *this*
flame ablaze. All my high hopes have fallen
low.
Oh my child, I never thought to see you married
amidst the spears and swords of Argos.
Give me the torch! As you whirl and spin, it is
dangerous and might fall.
I thought perhaps the agony of our plight would
bring you to your senses.
But no, you are still the same. Women of Troy!
Take the torches.
Weep tears in answer to her wedding songs.   350

CASSANDRA: Mother, put a wreath of victory upon my
head. Rejoice with me.
I am marrying a king! Lead me to him. If I falter,
take me to him by force.
Apollo is a prophet. Agamemnon, noble king of
the Greeks, will find me a more deadly bride

23

Than Helen ever was. I shall kill him. I shall
bring his house to ruin.
I will avenge the deaths of my father and my
brothers. But . . . no more now.
I will not tell of the axe that will fall upon my
neck and on another's, too . . .
Nor the killing of a mother, long after my mar-
riage . . .
Nor of the fall of the House of Atreus.
I am possessed, but for once I shall escape that
possession and will prove that Troy is more
Fortunate than all the Greeks.
The hunters of Helen, for the sake of that one
woman,
That one passion, have perished in the thou-
sands.
Their commander-in-chief, the clever Agamem-
non, killed the sweetest creature in the world,
His own daughter.
For the sake of those he hated most he sacrificed
the joyful heart of his house.
He gave in to his brother for *that* woman.
Never forget that she was willing and was not
taken by force!
From the moment they landed on these shores,
they began to die.
They were not defending their borders or their
towering cities.
Those whom the God of War struck down never
saw their children again.
Their bodies were not wrapped for death by the
loving hands of their wives.
They lie forever in alien soil. In Greece the mis-
ery was the same.
Widows died alone, old men walked childless
through their empty homes.
The sons they reared now served other men.

24

No one was left to pour libations of blood upon
their graves.
This is the glory of the Greek invasion. But it is
better to pass over their crimes in silence.
May my inner muse never sing an evil tale!
But the Trojans died for their country! What
more glorious fame than that?
Those cut down by the sword had friends to carry
their bodies home.
They were buried in the bosom of their native
earth,
Wrapped for death by hands that loved them.
And those Trojans that escaped a warrior's death
Spent their days at home with wives and children.
The Greeks had left such joys behind.
> Listen to me now. Hector died. It hurt so
> deeply. But he lives in fame.
He is a hero for all time. Without the Greek inva-
sion, this would not be.
Without their coming here, his virtues would
have died in silence.
Even Paris. Listen!
He coupled with the daughter of Zeus! Without
Helen, he would have been nothing.
His name would have died with him.
In the end it comes to this: a wise man will never
go to war.
But if war must come, then glory comes to the
good, even if they die.
The bad will live in infamy. Therefore, my
mother, do not weep for our country.
Do not weep for my virginity lost. I will couple
and I will kill the enemies of our house.

CHORUS: At times you seem to laugh at your pain. At
times you say things I do not understand.
Perhaps this comforts you.   400

25

TALTHYBIUS: It's good that it was Apollo made you mad. Otherwise you'd pay for this—sending my

Generals home with curses such as these.

It's true, though—the big people, the men that everyone thinks so brilliant,

They're no better than the nobodies. Take Agamemnon, all-powerful king of all Greece.

He's gone crazy over this mad woman.

I'm nothing. No money, nothing. But I'd never take a woman like that to my bed.

(to Cassandra) All right, you. You slandered the Greeks, you praised the Trojans.

But I know you're mad, so I'll let your words fly away in the wind.

Let it go. Come with me . . . you'll make a perfect bride for the king.

(to Hecuba) You! Be ready when Odysseus calls.

Penelope is a good woman by all accounts. You'll be her slave.

CASSANDRA: *You* are the slave and as vile as your trade!

We hate you, you pandering go-betweens, you men who slither between kings and countries!

Listen, you say my mother will live in the palace of Odysseus?

Apollo said to me that she will die here. But I remain silent about the shame.

Oh Odysseus is cursed! He does not know the terrors that face him.

The day will come when my pain, Troy's pain, will seem like joys of gold to him.

He lived here for ten years, hard years. For ten years more he will weep and groan.

He will go home, but alone, without friends.

He will face Charybdis, where the waters suck
and drain between the rocks.
Then the Cyclops, who eats human flesh in his
mountain cave.
Then Circe, who can turn heroes into swine. His
ship will founder on the deep.
He will succumb to the Lotus Eaters and the Holy
Cattle of the Sun.
The Cattle will take human voice and tell him his
tale of woe.
But enough! In the end he will descend alive to
hell, to Hades.
But when he escapes the clutches of the sea, he
will come home
To sorrows beyond number.
Enough of Odysseus, enough of his troubles.

(to Talthybius) Take me, march me off now!
I want to lie in the bed of my new husband, the
bed of Death.
Oh Agamemnon, mighty general of all the
Greeks!
You will be buried in shame, not in the sunlight,
but in the sly darkness of night.
Oh you seemed so mighty, so strong.
I, too, will die. Of course. I will be stripped naked
and my body thrown into a ravine,
Where winter floods foam and roar.
I will lie close to my dead husband, but wild ani-
mals will eat my flesh to the bone.
I was Apollo's priestess, Oh my God I loved you!
Here are the wreaths I wore for you whom I
loved. Here are the robes that I kissed in pride.
I will never again feast at your ritual table. Go,
go! I tear you from my skin.
My body is still pure. I give them to the whirling
winds.

27

Take them to you, Apollo, God of Prophecy!
Where is Agamemnon's ship? Where must I
    board? Quick, now, no time to lose.
A wind will come and fill your sails. I will be
    taken from my mother.
I am one of three Furies!
Goodbye, mother, do not weep.
    My country,
    My brothers already under the earth,
    My father that made me,
    I will be with you soon!
    But when I come below to you, I will come as
        a victor,
    The woman who destroyed our enemies,
    Destroyed the House of Atreus!

(Exeunt Talthybius and Cassandra. Hecuba collapses to the ground.)

CHORUS: You who have long looked after our
    Queen, raise her up again.
She has fallen, lies prostrate and silent on the
    ground. Raise her up!
She is old, frail . . . take her in your arms.

HECUBA: Do not touch me, my children. I want no
    help.
Let me lie where I have fallen. I had every reason
    to fall to the ground.
See what I suffer, have suffered, will suffer.
Oh you gods, help me!
But they will not help.
It is an empty ritual to call upon them when
    there is nothing left.
These are my last words to you.
Remember first my joy, my glory, and then think
    upon my pain.
I was a queen.

My husband was a king. I bore him noble chil-
   dren, the best of the best of Troy.
I saw them die in battle with the Greeks. I cut my
   hair in mourning over their graves.
Priam, their father—no one *told* me of his death.
   I saw it, with my own eyes.
I saw them cut his throat over the hearth.
Hah! The hearth of Zeus the Protector.
I saw my city die. I saw my virgin daughters,
   raised to marry the princes of the kingdom,
I saw them taken to be the brides of Death.
I have no hope that I will see them again, or they
   me.
And now this end, this crown of all my woes:
I go to Greece.
In my old age I will be a slave.
I am old, but they will not care. They will make
   me watch the keys at the gate.
Me! The mother of Hector!
Perhaps I will have to bake bread and rest my
   wrinkled back upon the dirt warmed by the
   oven.
I who once slept in the soft bed of the palace.
My body is battered. I will be dressed in rags, in
   tatters.
I once wore the robes of a queen.
But this is my now, this is my tomorrow.
I am condemned by the lust of one woman.
   Helen.

Cassandra, Cassandra! My daughter, my
   daughter!
A god made you mad, a god made you pure.
A god sent you to death.
Polyxena, Polyxena! My daughter, my daughter!
   Where are you? Where are you?
I had so many children.

Now, no son, no daughter live to help me, their
    mother, their mother.
So why do you raise me from the earth?
There is no hope.
Take me in your arms.
Once I walked soft on Trojan silk.
Now take me to some stony hollow in the
    ground, let hard rocks be my pillow.
I am a slave. Let me lie upon the ground and end
    my life in tears.
Oh the favorites of Fortune! Look on them, for
    they will never find happiness this side of
    death!

510   CHORUS: Sing to me of Troy, my Muse!
            Sing a strange tale of woe.
            Sing to me of tears.
            Sing to me of death.

The song I now sing, I sing for Troy.
A beast, wooden, four-footed, destroyed us.
The Greeks left the horse at our gates
Covered in gold.
The rattle of the armor within touched the heav-
    ens.
All the people of Troy on every corner cried out,
"Come, come! Your troubles are over!
Lead into our city this creature, sacred to the Vir-
    gin of Troy,
Virgin daughter of Zeus!"
All the maidens, all the old men left their homes.
They sang, they laughed as they embraced their
    unknown death.

Every son, every daughter of Troy rushed to the
    gates
To honor the immortal virgin,
To give to the goddess this treacherous gift

30

Of mountain pine,
With its belly full of Greeks.

They threw ropes around it, as if it were some
    great black ship
They were dragging to the sea.
They brought it to the stony temple of the god-
    dess, Pallas, virgin Pallas.
They set it on the sacred ground. . . .
There we lost the blood of our life, the blood of
    our land.
They loved the work, they laughed. But then
    darkness descended.
In Troy the flutes shrilled. There was dancing,
    there were songs.
The air was filled with the rhythm of pounding
    feet, with the singing of virgins.
Everywhere torches flared.
Even deep in the recesses of houses where people
    slept
There was a warm glow of comfort.
That night I too sang in the choirs before the
    temple of the Virgin of the Mountains,
The daughter of Zeus.

And then suddenly . . . all the city rang with cries
    of terror!
Little children grabbed in fear the robes of their
    mothers.
The God of War burst from the belly of the
    beast.
Pallas, Pallas Athena had her will!
Trojan blood flowed, ran on every altar.
In their lonely beds young women cut off their
    hair . . .
Crowns of triumph for the Greeks,
Offerings of grief for the Trojans.

Hecuba! Look! Andromache! On a peasant's cart,
Astyanax in her weeping arms.
Where are they taking you, sweet, sad woman,
where?
Astyanax is holding onto her for dear life. Oh
Hector, this is your son! Why do they do this?
They pile your armor, pile the spoils of Troy
upon this cart. And the son of Achilles will
make
Them shine on the walls of his temples, far far
from Troy.

[The following interchange was sung as a kind of
formal public mourning, an ululation.]

ANDROMACHE: The Greeks, the Greeks make me
575   their slave.

HECUBA: Ahh, ahh . . . weep for me!

ANDROMACHE: Why do you weep? Weep for me.

HECUBA: Ahh, ahh, ahh . . .

ANDROMACHE: The grief is mine!

HECUBA: Oh God, Oh Zeus!

ANDROMACHE: The misery is mine!

HECUBA: Oh my children!

ANDROMACHE: Dead, dead, dead.

HECUBA: Gone is the glory, gone is Troy.

ANDROMACHE: The pain!

HECUBA: Gone my children, gone my princes.

ANDROMACHE: Ahh, ahh . . . weep for me!

HECUBA: Ahh, yes, weep. Weep for what I have lost.

ANDROMACHE: Ahh, weep for me.

HECUBA: The glory, the riches . . .

ANDROMACHE: . . . of my city . . .

HECUBA: . . . gone—in smoke.

ANDROMACHE: Come to me, my husband!

HECUBA: He is dead. My son is dead. Weep for me.

ANDROMACHE: Come, save your wife!

HECUBA: Come, my husband, whom the Greeks cut
down to their shame . . .

ANDROMACHE: Father of my Hector! Priam, old, great
Priam.

HECUBA: Come send me to my sleep, the sleep of
death.

ANDROMACHE: Our longings are deep.

HECUBA: Our griefs are deep.

ANDROMACHE: For our city is dead.

HECUBA: Grief upon grief.

ANDROMACHE: Our city is dead. The evil minds of the
gods killed it.
Your son, Paris, should have died at birth.
But he escaped and, for the love of an evil
woman, destroyed our city.
Pallas, Virgin, before your temples the bodies of
our dead lie soaked in blood!
The birds will eat them.
This is the end.
Troy is a slave.

HECUBA: Oh my country, Oh my country!   600

ANDROMACHE: I weep as I leave you.

HECUBA: The end, the bitter end is here.

33

ANDROMACHE: I leave my home where my baby was born.

HECUBA: Oh my babies, you have gone!
　　You have left your mother!
　　The city is an empty shell.
　　Now, only the sadness of the dirge!
　　The grief shrilled in the night!
　　The tears!
　　Cataracts of tears!
　　But the dead cannot weep.
　　They have forgotten grief.

[This next section is spoken.]

CHORUS: The pain is deep, but tears are a sweet solace. Lamentation soothes the soul.

ANDROMACHE: Mother of Hector, he who was the brave killer of so many Greeks,
　　Do you see what they do?

HECUBA: I see the power of the gods.
　　Some they raise to towering glory, others they make grovel in the dust of the earth.

ANDROMACHE: We are led away, trussed like stolen cattle, my son and me! Once we were kings.
　　Now we are slaves. The change hangs heavy on my heart.

HECUBA: Necessity is a goddess. She is inescapable.
　　Cassandra was this moment torn from my arms.

ANDROMACHE: Ahh . . . another Ajax for your daughter? Another man who will rape her?
　　But I know that is not all . . .

HECUBA: Not all? I have pains that I cannot count, grief mounts upon grief.

ANDROMACHE: Polyxena, your daughter, is dead.

She was murdered at the tomb of Achilles, a life given to the lifeless dead.

HECUBA: Oh where will my grief end? This is what Talthybius meant.
He spoke in darkness, but the truth now finds the light.

ANDROMACHE: I saw her myself. I got off this cart. I covered her with her robes.
I beat my breast for the dead.

HECUBA: Oh my child, brutally murdered! Oh god, Oh god, the shame of her death!

ANDROMACHE: Her death was a clean death, but I who live on, live on condemned to pain.

HECUBA: Death and life are not the same, my child. Death is nothingness, life means hope.

ANDROMACHE: But the dead are as if they had never been born.
It is better to die than to live a life of pain. The dead feel no sorrow.
But a man who was once happy, when sorrow comes, longs for the joys he once knew.
Polyxena is dead. It is as if she had never known life. She feels no sorrow.
I lived a life seeking respect. The more I won, the more I had to lose.
In Hector's house I worked hard. I won the reputation of a virtuous wife.
I stayed within the confines of his house and never ventured out.
I never could be accused of being unfaithful to my husband. Slander could not touch me.
I did not let into my house the tongues of gossiping women.

35

I am what I am: a woman of honor. I needed
   nothing.
My tongue was still, my face serene when Hector
   was with me.
I knew how to persuade him and I knew when to
   let him tell me I was wrong.
   This reputation that I earned reached the ears
      of the Greeks. It has ruined me!
When I was captured, the son of Achilles wanted
   me for his wife.
I will be a slave in the house of the man who
   murdered my husband.
If I forget Hector, the man I loved, if I open my
   heart to my new master,
I will be seen as a traitor to the dead.
But If I remain faithful to my husband's love, I
   will be hated by the man whose slave I am.
They say that a single night in a new man's bed
   softens the loathing, but not for me.
I despise the woman who gets remarried, who, in
   the passionate arms of another,
Forgets the love of her first man.
Even when two horses are separated, the old part-
   ner will pull reluctantly.
And they are brutes without reason, without
   speech. We are human beings!
Oh sweet Hector, you were all the husband I ever
   wanted!
You were wise, noble, rich, brave, a great man!
I came to you a virgin from my father's house.
My bed was pure, you were the first to enter.
Now you are dead and I am being sent to Greece,
   a slave.
(to Hecuba) You weep for Polyxena, but is her
   death worse than the pain of my life?
Hope that lives in the heart of the living lives not
   in me.

670

36

I have no hope, no comfort left in my mind. It is finished.

CHORUS: Your grief I share. As you weep, I too weep for what I know will fall upon me.

HECUBA: I have never been aboard a ship. But I have heard stories, seen pictures.
I know what happens.
If the storm the sailors face is not too great, they fight to save themselves.
One man takes the helm, another hauls the sails, another bails the water out of the boat.
But if the waves mountain over them, if the storm crashes down upon them,
They submit, they give their bodies to the mercy of the waves.
Like them, I am washed by sorrow. The waves beat me down and I submit.
I am silent now. I need no more words. The waves of misery have beaten me down.
The gods have drowned me in sorrow.
My child, think no more of Hector. Your tears will not save him now.
You have a new lord, respect him. Make him love your beauty, your sweetness.
If you do, you will find happiness again.
Those who love you will find happiness again.
And this grandson of mine will live to be a hero for Troy once again.
Someday his sons will return. And Troy will live again, be a city again.
But here is Talthybius . . . there is no respite. What now, what now. . . ?   700

TALTHYBIUS: Andromache, Hector's wife, forgive me.
Hector was the bravest of all the Trojans, forgive me.

37

What I have to say is not of my choosing.
The Greeks have . . . the sons of Atreus have . . .

ANDROMACHE: Tell me! I feel a song of grief welling
in my heart already.

TALTHYBIUS: This boy here . . . They have decided . . .
I can't do it, say it . . .

ANDROMACHE: What! Are we not to be slaves together?

TALTHYBIUS: No Greek will be his master.

ANDROMACHE: Will they leave him here? Last rem-
nant of the Trojan house?

TALTHYBIUS: I do not know how to tell you. It hurts
to speak.

ANDROMACHE: I thank you for your kindness. I fear
your news.

TALTHYBIUS: They are going to kill your child. Your
grief dies there.

ANDROMACHE: No! No! My slave-marriage is as nothing now!

TALTHYBIUS: Odysseus persuaded them all in the as-
sembly that this was right.

ANDROMACHE: Ahh god! Ahh god! I cannot bear my
pain!

TALTHYBIUS: He said that a son of such a man as his
father should not be allowed to grow old.

ANDROMACHE: May his words curse his own children!

TALTHYBIUS: They will throw your son from the towers of Troy.
Come . . . let things take their course. Be wise in
the midst of pain.

Give the boy up to me. Be brave! Let the agony
rest in your sorrowing heart.

You can do nothing, you have nothing left!
There is no one here to help. Look around
you.

Troy is dead, your husband is dead, you are a
slave. We can bind you, tie you up.

You are alone. There is nothing you can do. Why
humiliate yourself further?

Why make your pain worse?

All right, let me warn you. Don't curse the
Greeks!

If you say anything to make them angry, this boy
may get no burial.

I mean it! No one will be allowed to weep for
him. Silence! Silence! Make the best of it.

Then you might be allowed to bury him. And the
Greeks might be kinder toward you.

ANDROMACHE: My sweet child, I love you more than
anything.

You will be taken from me and I can do nothing.
You will be killed by our enemies.

Your father was brave, a hero beyond heroes. And
this simple fact has killed you.

His greatness flowered. You will be cut down at
the root.

My tears flow now for that marriage long ago.
Oh Hector!

My baby, are you weeping too? Do you know what
is happening?

You hold on to me, you hold me tight. Do you
understand?

You are like a little bird beneath my wing. Your
father cannot save you now.

He cannot kill them all, spear in hand. He is in
his grave. There is no one left to help.

39

The once-great power of Troy is dead. You will
    fall through the air, my son.
The pain is unspeakable!
You will crash hard against the hard ground and
    your neck will break
And your breath will leave your body.
I love you, my baby! I love the scent of your living
    body in my arms.
I love, quite simply, to hold you.
My breasts gave you milk so that you could grow
    into a man. In vain.
I wrapped you in the clothes of a child. In vain.
I screamed in pain at your birth. In vain.
Kiss me, now. Kiss your mother for the last time.
    Kiss me.
I gave you life. Put your arms around me, put
    your lips on mine!
    You Greeks, you think of yourselves as civilized.
        But you behave like beasts.
Your instinct is torture. You will murder an inno-
    cent child!
Oh Helen, you are not Zeus's daughter!
You are the bastard child of Hate and Murder
    and Death,
The child of every monster bred of this earth!
    You are no daughter of Zeus.
Never will I let my lips say it.
Your life was the death of Greeks beyond num-
    ber, Trojans beyond number.
I curse your very being. Your eyes made light but
    brought darkness on the earth.
(she gives her child to Talthybius) Take him, take my
    baby.
Hurl him to his death, if that is what you want.
Eat his living flesh, if that is what you want.
It is the gods who are killing us. I have no power.
    My son will die.

40

Cover me now, wrap me in robes. I go to the
   ships.
It is time to be married. For my son is dead.

CHORUS: I weep for Troy.
   One woman made these deaths. Helen.
   She made the graves of thousands her bed.   780

TALTHYBIUS: Come, poor child. Leave your mother's
   loving arms.
   You will go now to the highest citadel that once
      was Troy. There you must die.
   That is what they said. *(to a guard)* Take him!
   I'm not very good at this. You need a man with a
      heart of stone. It's too painful . . . I hate it.

(exeunt Talthybius and Men)

HECUBA: There is nothing now. My child, you have
   gone.
   There is nothing now. No justice.
   All I have left is to beat my head, tear the flesh of
      my breasts, and weep.
   I have nothing now but grief for my city, a grief
      that crashes down, that crashes down . . .

(Andromache is taken away and Hecuba collapses)

CHORUS: Telamon! You were the first to kill the
   kings of Troy.   800
   Telamon, King of Salamis, where bees hum in the
      air!
   Telamon, king of the island where the olive
      shoots grow green in the sun!
   Where Athena's green eyes sweetened the fruit.
   Telamon, you screamed God's courage to the
      wind and you destroyed Troy!
   Oh destroyed Troy.
   Listen, now.
   He brought with him the best of men.

41

All he had lost were some stolen cattle.
But in a fury . . . Oh listen, now . . .
He crossed the seas.
He anchored in the bay where Troy lives.
He made fast the ropes.
He took his weapons, sharp arrows.
Laomedon was King of Troy.
But he was destined for death.
Apollo had built the walls,
Apollo had made them tall and true.
But Telamon set them afire, burnt them down.
What we see today is a second death.
The armies of the Greeks have murdered twice.

Ganymede! You were the son of Troy's king!
You walk in soft light.
You kiss the lips of the golden cups
Of Zeus, your loving lord.
But it means nothing.
You cannot help us now.
Your mother earth is in flames.
Her beaches weep.
You can hear the sea scream,
Like birds when their young die.
Weeping for husbands,
Weeping for children,
Weeping for mothers lost.
Once you bathed in waters warm.
Once you wrestled in the sun.
Once you ran in the wind.
Nothing now.
There in Olympus you smile
And live in peace.
Here below the Greeks smile
And kill
With the razors of their spears.

Love, Eros, Love!

Long ago you came to the House of Dardanus,
Old King of Troy.
The gods disapproved.
Troy was loved then,
Oh Troy was loved.
Zeus . . . O how can I speak of his shame?
But this day when Dawn kissed our earth
With her white wings,
When her light that we love touched us,
We saw blood.
We saw the death of our earth.
How can we understand the gods?
Here, here is where Dawn found the lover of her
    bed,
Made her children,
Soared into the sky
In a chariot of four blazing stars.
But now we are nothing.
Troy was golden once.
And now is only dust.

(enter Menelaus) 860

MENELAUS: The sun is beautiful today! I bask in it!
    Today I will get my wife back.
I came to Troy—people thought this, but they
    were wrong—not to get my wife back,
But to meet, face to face, the man who took her
    from me.
He's dead now, thanks be to God.
We Greeks stuck our spears right in them and the
    country's dead.
I am here now to take the Woman of Sparta
    home. I call her that . . . I can't speak her
    name.
She was my wife. Once. She's in there some-
    where, with the other Trojan women.

43

Those that fought this exhausting war to get her back have given her to me—to put to death.
Or, if I choose not to kill her, to take her back to Argos.
I've made up my mind: I will not decide what to do with her here in Troy.
I will wait. I'll put her on board ship and take her to Greece.
Then I'll hand her over to those whose loved ones died over here.
They can take their vengeance. They will kill her.
So, men, go inside and bring her here! Drag her here by her lethal hair!
When the winds are right, we'll take her back to Greece.

HECUBA: *(rising up)* Oh Zeus! You who support the earth and are by earth supported,
Hear my prayers!
Zeus, Zeus, whatever you are, you who defy the striving of our knowledge,
Whether you are the Law of Necessity in Nature or the Law of Reason in mankind,
Hear my prayers! You are everywhere, you move in silence!
You rule human life with the power of Justice!

MENELAUS: What is this? You pray in such a strange manner.

HECUBA: I praise you, Menelaus, for your decision to kill your wife. But leave, now.
Do not look on her. Desire will make a slave of you. She enslaves all who look upon her.
She destroys cities, she burns down homes. Such is her evil magic!
I know her. You know her. All her victims know her.

44

HELEN: Menelaus! If you intended to terrify me, you succeeded.
Your men laid their rough hands on me and dragged me from the tents.
I understand that you might hate me, but I still must ask,
What do you and the Greek army intend to do with me?

MENELAUS: We did not discuss your case specifically.
But the army has given you to me, the man you wronged, to have you put to death.

HELEN: Will you let me speak in my defense?
I can prove that my death, if I am to be killed, will be unjust.

MENELAUS: I did not come here to argue, I came to kill you!

HECUBA: Let her speak. You must not kill her without a hearing.
But let me be the prosecutor. I know the case.
You have no knowledge of all the wicked things she did in Troy.
I will speak to the point. I will cover everything.
I will prove that her death would be just, and I will leave her no means of escape.

MENELAUS: This will take more time than I have to spare. But if she wants to speak, let her.
Let me be clear—I grant this not as a favor to her, but so she will have to listen to you.

HELEN: *(to Menelaus)* You think of me as your enemy.
So I doubt that you will respond favorably to my arguments,
Whether you think they are good or bad.

But I think I know what charges you will bring
    against me and I will answer them.
    First, it was this woman here who started all
        our troubles when she gave birth to Paris.
Second, it was Priam who destroyed both Troy
    and me. He should have killed his son at
    birth.
He knew what the omens meant.
He dreamed that his son would burn Troy to the
    ground: that was the truth.
But that was just the beginning. This is what fol-
    lowed.
Paris sat in judgment of the beauty of the three
    goddesses.
Athena offered him the leadership of the Trojan
    army that would overthrow Greece.
Hera promised him Asia and Europe if he chose
    her.
Aphrodite merely talked to him of me, told him
    of my extraordinary beauty,
Promised me to him if he would choose her over
    the other goddesses.
Remember the consequences of that! Aphrodite
    won.
Now think of what my coupling with Paris did for
    Greece:
She was not conquered by barbarians, she did not
    face them in battle,
Nor submit to their domination.
But Greece's good fortune was the ruin of me.
I was bartered for my beauty and now I am re-
    viled.
But I should be given a crown to wear for what I
    did!
Perhaps you will say I am avoiding the main
    point:

Why did I leave your house in the secrecy of
    darkness?
This woman's son, Paris, or Alexander if you pre-
    fer, was an evil guest.

(2) He came into our home with a most powerful
    goddess by his side.
But you, my unworthy husband, were not there to
    protect me!
You left that man behind in your house. You had

(3) gone to Crete and I was alone.
    But enough of that. I will ask myself the next
        question. I will not ask you.
Was I sane when I ran away from home with a

(4) stranger, abandoned my country, my family?
    No.
But blame Aphrodite for my insanity! Men
    should be greater than Zeus ... he is king of
    the gods, but even he is Aphrodite's slave. So
    do not blame me.   slave of love
    There is one more point which might provide
        you with a false argument against me:
When Paris was dead and buried, why did I not
    leave his house and return to you and the
    Greek army? The gods had no more interest in
    my love affairs.
Well, that is exactly what I tried to do. I have wit-
    nesses.
The guards on the towers, the watchmen, saw me

(5) time and time again trying to escape,
Secretly trying to let myself down on ropes from
    the battlements.
So, my husband, how could you justify my death?
First of all, I was taken against my will.

(6) Second, what I have done for my people has
    made me a slave, not a victor crowned in
    glory.

47

So, be greater than Zeus, if that's your will. But it
    reeks of stupidity.

CHORUS: Oh my Queen, defend your children, de-
    fend your country!
    She speaks well, but kill her words. She is elo-
    quent but wicked.
965   That is a combination to be feared!

HECUBA: First of all, I shall speak of the goddesses.
    I shall defend them, show that her charges
    against them are unjust.
    I do not believe that Hera and Athena were,
    quite bluntly,
    So stupid as to give Argos to barbarians or Athens
    to Troy
    Just to win a beauty contest on Mount Ida.
    Why should Hera, Goddess Supreme, have
    longed for beauty? She was married to Zeus!
    Was she looking for something better?
    Was Virgin Athena looking for a husband
    amongst the available gods?
    She was, and ever will be, a virgin.
    Her father, Zeus, granted her that gift as she wept
    before him.
    Do not make the gods fools to cover your own
    wickedness!
    Intelligent men will laugh at your arguments.
    You say that Aphrodite came with my son to your
    home, to the palace of Menelaus. Why?
    Could she not have sat comfortably on Mount
    Olympus and simply whisked you away, Argos
    and all, to Troy?
    My son was handsome beyond all belief.
    You looked on him and your heart was filled with
    the lust of Aphrodite.
    Men blame her for every mindless act that they
    commit.

Her name begins with "A"; it stands for amorality
. . . animal lust.

You saw my son, dressed in gleaming gold, an ex-
otic barbarian. And you lost your mind.

In Argos you had been a simple wife. Few ser-
vants. But you loved the thought of Troy.

No more the thin life of Sparta. Gold! Rivers of
opulence flowing over you here in my city!

Sparta's halls, Menelaus's home, were not
enough to satisfy your lust for luxury.

And now to your next point. You said you were
taken by force, by my son.

No one in Sparta heard one single sound of
protest. Did you scream?

Your brother Castor was there. Your brother Pol-
lux, not yet a star in the heavens, was there.

They were strong, but still not a sound from you!

Then when you came to Troy and the Greeks
were in pursuit and the bloodbath had started,

Whenever reports came to the city of some suc-
cess of Menelaus, you would praise him.

You would torment my son. You would pit him
against your husband, the great Menelaus.

But if we, the Trojans, were victorious, Menelaus
was as nothing.

You looked only in the eyes of Fate, and you did
not care about your honor or your virtue.

You simply waited.

And then you say you tried to escape, tried to
save your skin by ropes hung from the battlements.

You wanted to escape? Hah!

Why did you not tie those ropes around your
neck and hang yourself?

Why did you not sharpen a knife as any good wife
would have done

Out of respect for her former husband?

49

And yet . . . and yet . . . I talked to you often.

I said: "Get away, now! My sons can find other
brides. I will help you to escape!

I will get you to the Greek fleet! Let us end this
hideous war!"

But this meant nothing to you. You were making
love in the House of Paris.

You wanted barbarians to be your slaves, you
loved it, you reveled in it.

And now you come out here dressed in the trap-
pings of your lust.

You and Menelaus are here together. I hate you!
You should have left here in rags.

You should be lying on the ground in fear.

You should have your hair cut short in grief.

You should not speak to us like this.

You should be silent and full of shame.

Menelaus! Hear what I must say to end this
cross-examination!

Greece must be crowned by her death. She must
die! Let that be the law.

Death to every woman who betrays her husband!

1030   CHORUS: Menelaus, this demands revenge.

Remember the honor of your house!

You have proved yourself to your enemies, now
prove yourself to your countrymen

And do not succumb to a woman!

MENELAUS: I have listened and I agree. She left my
bed for another man.

She chose to do it.

She uses Aphrodite's name in her defense. Non-
sense!

Take her away! Let the men stone her to death!

Let one minute pay for ten years of Greek an-
guish.

You dishonored me and you will pay!

HELEN: Do not kill me! I hold your knees in suppli-
cation! Do not kill me!
It was not I! The gods are to blame! Forgive me!

HECUBA: She caused the death of all the men who
came here. Do not betray them!
Remember them, remember their children!

MENELAUS: *(to Hecuba)* Woman, speak no more! She
is nothing now. Men, take her on board!

HECUBA: Do not let her set foot on your ship!

MENELAUS: Why? Is she too much of a burden? Will
she sink the ship?

HECUBA: You loved her once, you will love her again.

MENELAUS: That depends on the lover.
But I grant your wish. She will not sail on my
ship.
And when she comes to Argos, she will be pun-
ished.
A slave's death for a woman of shame. She will
show all women that chastity is their duty.
Not an easy thing to achieve . . .
But her death will strike terror in their hearts,
fools though they may be and worse.
Yet they might learn from this.

CHORUS: Zeus, you have betrayed us!
Zeus, you have deserted Troy!
Zeus, you have made us the slaves of Greeks!
These were your altars, your temples.
Here flesh and incense and myrrh
Sent the perfumes of our prayers to you!

You did not hear our prayers.
You have abandoned Troy, this sacred spot.
Where ivy clothes the valleys of Mount Ida,
Where the streams swell with mountain snow,

Where the sky ends in the sun,
And the light kisses the holy earth.
There are no more sacrifices.
No more the laughter of the dance.
No more the flickering ceremonies in the dark.
When the gilded statues of the gods
Shone bright and bathed in mystery.

At each full moon we worshiped you in Troy.
No more, no more.
You sit there, Lord Zeus, on your throne in
    heaven.
Do you care? Do you care?
My city is nothing now.
My city is nothing but ashes.

Oh my husband!
You are a ghost with no grave.
Unwashed, unburied, you lie lonely in the sand.
I must speed across the sea
To Argos, where the horses race in the sun.
Where the walls of Cyclops touch the sky.
Here my children huddle at Troy's gate.
They weep beyond grief,
They call out:
"Mother! Mother!
I will see you no more!
The Greeks have torn me from your arms!
They will put me on their black ships.
They will take me to Salamis,
Or to the isthmus that looks upon two seas,
Or to the hated land of Sparta!"

1100   I have a curse.
When Menelaus sails,
When his ship is in mid-sea,
May a bolt of lightning split the decks!
Let the Aegean Sea be his death!

For he carries me from Troy
To be a slave in Greece.
What greater grief could there be?

But Helen, Oh Zeus's daughter,
She smiles before her mirrors of gold
As a virgin smiles at her reflection.

Let him never reach Sparta!
Let him never reach the home of his fathers!
Let him never again see the city of Pitana
Or the Gates of Bronze!
He has taken with him this wife,
This evil wife.
She shamed Greece.
She brought sorrow to Troy,
Where the River Simois now weeps tears of pain.

(enter Talthybius with the body of Astyanax on Hector's shield)

CHORUS: Oh God, Oh God! My grief was deep and
new and living within me.
But now there is more. Look, look, you Trojan
women, on the body of Astyanax!
The Greeks have killed him! They threw him
from the battlements to a cruel death.

TALTHYBIUS: Hecuba, there is one ship left. It will
soon set sail for Phthia.
It will be carrying the prizes that Neoptolemus takes
home.
He has already left after hearing of troubles at
home. Acastus has banished him.
He had no time to lose. He has taken Andromache
with him.
I must confess, she made me weep when she left.
She moaned her grief for her country, for her Hector.

53

She begged her new masters to let her bury her
child, your Hector's son.
They had killed him by throwing him off the high
walls of Troy.
He lies here on Hector's shield. She begged Neoptolemus not to take it with him.
These brass plates saved Hector's life for a while,
terrified us Greeks.
She said, "Do not take it to Greece and put it on a
wall beside the bed where I must lie with you!
I could not bear that. I am his mother.
Let me bury my child in a coffin of cedar or a tomb
of stone!
Let me give the body to Hecuba. Let her wrap it in
soft cloth and flowers.
Oh give her leave to do all that she has strength left
to do!"
She has gone. Neoptolemus was in a hurry. She
could not bury her own son.
So. When you have dressed the corpse, we must
cover it with dust and set sail.
You have to hurry. I saved you a little work.
When we crossed the River Scamander, I washed
the body, washed the blood from the wounds.
So . . . I have to go. I'll start breaking the ground
for his grave.
If we do this together, it'll save time. The ship is
waiting and we must set out for home.

HECUBA: Lay the shield on the ground. I know its
shape. I know it and love it.
And it makes me weep.
Greeks, Greeks! You love war more than you love
being human. —no respect for the body.
What makes you afraid of this baby in my arms?
You had killed and you killed again.
Were you afraid that he would rise from the ashes
of Troy, make us great again?

54

[handwritten margin notes:]
1150
death of
new
grandson

does not understand
why they had to kill the child
brutality of war.

You are, in the end, cowards. Troy is dead, is
  nothing now.
But you were afraid of this child, this . . . this
  baby.
Hector and men in their thousands could not
  save us. But you were afraid of this child.
There was no reason, none.
My sweet baby, you had the worst of deaths.
If you had died fighting to save our city, if you
  had enjoyed just being young,
If you had been in love and married, if you had
  been a prince—one of the chosen divine—,
You would have been happy . . . if there is such a
  thing as happiness.
As it was, you knew these things only in the
  dream of your young eyes.
You looked but you did not become a king.
Oh poor child, the walls that were yours, the walls
  that Apollo built,
Have battered your skull, ripped the hair from
  your head, the curls that your mother kissed.
My heart breaks when I see death grinning in
  your broken mouth.
I touch your hands, limp and cold, and I remem-
  ber your father.
I touch your lips and remember the child-voice
  that sang in my heart. Silent now.
You lied, my baby, you used to climb onto my bed
  and say,
"Mother, ahh Mother! I'm going to cut a curl
  from my hair, a big one, and I'll bring all my
  friends and we'll put it on your grave. And
  we'll all say goodbye and we love you."
But that was not for you. It was for me.
I, the old woman without a country now, without
  children now. I will bury you, my baby child.
I remember the kisses, the nights you spent in my
  arms, my love for you.

55

Nothing now.
What will some poet write on your tomb?:
  The Greeks in Fear of You Did Shake
  And Therefore Did Your Sweet Life Take.
Forever those words will shame the Greek world.
My child, your prince's legacy of gold is no more.
Your father's shield of bronze will carry you to
  your tomb, this shield that protected my son.
Oh Hector, your strong arm holds it no more!
I can see the marks of your hand upon the
  leather, I can see the salt of your sweat upon
  the rim where you pressed it to your beard and
  fought to the death.

1200

Come, I know there is not much left for us now.
  But dress this child for death.

Life a continual Challenge. No certainty.

Fate has robbed us of gilded clothes, but what I
  have I will give.
The man who believes that Fortune smiles on
  him is a fool. Fortune knows no reason.
She is mad, she shifts from mood to mood, gives
  this, takes that.
Never is human life serene.

CHORUS: Look, they are bringing what little is left of
  Troy! Cold raiment for the dead.

HECUBA: My child, you did not win a battle in your
  chariot or with your bow.
  But for Troy's sake, for Troy, I, the mother of
  your father, wrap you in glory,
  These poor rags of glory. Helen was the thief that
  took it all,
  Your palace, your kingdom, and your life.

CHORUS: *(sings)* I am beyond grief
  My heart breaks.
  Hector, Oh Hector,
  Prince of a dead land.

HECUBA: These are the robes, torn now, once the pride of Troy,
Which you would have worn on your wedding day. A prince marrying an Asian princess.
I lay them on your body.
Hector's shield!
Father of victories beyond number, take this simple offering of flowers.
Hector's shield! You cannot die, you will live with the dead.
Odysseus won his prize of armor, but he will live only in the memory of shame.

CHORUS: *(sung)* Alas, alas!
The earth will take this child into her breast.
And we must weep.
Mother, Oh Mother, mourn for him!

HECUBA: *(sings)* Alas!

CHORUS: Weep for the dead!

HECUBA: My heart breaks.

CHORUS: My heart breaks too. There is no end.

HECUBA: *(speaking)* I wrap your wounds, but I cannot heal.
I am no doctor when the disease is death.
When you move amongst the dead, your father will take care of you.

CHORUS: Strike your heads, strike!
Beat your breasts to the rhythm of grief!

HECUBA: *(speaking)* Oh Trojan women . . .

CHORUS: Why do you cry aloud like that? We are yours. Speak to us!

HECUBA: After this life, there is nothing. Eternal grief, perhaps.

Eternal hate for Troy, a city hated beyond others.
We have slaughtered cattle in their hundreds as
  gifts to the gods.
For nothing.
Why did not a god take me, bury me in the earth
  so I would never have had a name?
Go, bury the body. Put it in a poor grave. Hell
  will be satisfied.
It doesn't matter to the dead that the rituals are
  simple.
It is only the living who are ashamed.

(they take the body away as the Chorus sings a dirge)

CHORUS: I weep for your mother.
  I weep for her hopes for you.
  I weep for a life splintered to the bone.
  You were a prince.
  The world envied you.
  And the world saw you die,
  Broken into inhuman pieces.

Ahh, ahh! I see fire consuming the walls of Troy!
I see human flesh writhing in the flames!
This is the next terror of our lives.

(enter Talthybius)

TALTHYBIUS: You were given orders to set fire to
  Priam's city.
  Begin! Troy must be a city of ashes.
  Then we can go home, go home happy.
  Trojan women! I have two orders: when the trum-
  pets sound,
  You women will march to the ships.
  Then . . . Hecuba, oh I pity you . . . you must go
  with these men whom Odysseus has sent.
  You are the slave that he won. He will take you
  from Troy.

HECUBA: It is the end. My sorrows peak and fall into
    the abyss of grief.
  I leave my country, I see my city in flames. My
    legs are weak, but I must press on.
  Oh let me say goodbye to my city, my sad, once-
    glorious city!
  Troy, once so great in the world that was not
    Greek,
  Now your name and your fame will be buried in
    your dust!
  You are ashes now and we are slaves. Oh Gods!
    But why do I call upon them?
  They have never heard my cries nor my prayers.
    Come, let me die in the fire.
  Let the flames that kill my city kill me.

TALTHYBIUS: I pity you. Grief makes you mad.
  Take her away! Do it quickly. Odysseus wants his
    prize. Give her to him!

(exit Talthybius)

[From here to the end, everything was sung.]

HECUBA: Ahh, ahh, ahh! Troy is in flames! The
    citadel burns.
  The houses are wreathed in fire.
  The very walls are consumed.

CHORUS: This was where we were born.
  And my defeated country now is dying,
  In smoke that drifts to heaven in the wind.
  Rich palaces are ravaged by the spear
  And by the flames of death.   1300

HECUBA: This is where I gave birth and reared my
    children.

CHORUS: Ahh, ahh!

59

HECUBA: Listen, my children!
  In the silence beneath the earth,
  Hear your mother!

CHORUS: Your grief will touch the dead!

HECUBA: Yes, I call to them
  As I lay my tired limbs
  Upon the earth.
  I beat the ground with my hands.
  I will speak to their silence.

CHORUS: We now kneel upon this earth.
  We call upon our husbands,
  Buried here so deep.

HECUBA: We are being taken from our homes . . .

CHORUS: Oh God! I hear your pain!

HECUBA: . . . to where we must be a slave.

CHORUS: Far from this land which gave us birth.

HECUBA: Oh Priam, my husband!
  Dead, dead,
  No grave for you,
  No friends.
  At least you do not share
  My suffering.

CHORUS: Yes, darkness covered his eyes.
  The darkness of death,
  Peace.
  But I curse those who killed him.

HECUBA: I see the temple of my gods,
  The city of my love . . .

CHORUS: Ahh, ahh!

HECUBA: . . . in flames!
  Destroyed by the savagery of the spear!

CHORUS: Soon the towers will fall.
  Our Mother Earth and your ashes
  Will become one.
  And your name for the rest of time
  Will be silence.

HECUBA: The smoke and the ashes begin to cloud
    the sky.
  The wings of dust cover the city that was my
    home.

CHORUS: Troy will be no more.
  Her name will die forever.
  Fate moves on relentless,
  Troy is dead!

HECUBA: Did you see,
  Oh did you see?
  Did you hear?

CHORUS: The sound of the city
  Falling in ruins.

HECUBA: Nothing but ruins.
  Ruins everywhere.

CHORUS: The city is no more.

HECUBA: I quake with fear,
  My limbs tremble.

  But lead me to where I must go.
  We will walk on.
  We will walk on.
  Into a life of slavery without end.

CHORUS: My city is no more.
  But we will walk on.
  We will walk on.

  The Greek fleet waits.

Even w/ great tragedy she must continue, up to fates, designs & the divine will.